No One Can Stem the Tide

No One Can Stem the Tide

the Tide

Selected Poems 1931–1991

Jane Tyson Clement

PLOUGH PUBLISHING HOUSE

811.54
c b26 n

Cover art:
Andrew Wyeth, "Wind from the Sea" (tempera, 1947).
Copyright © Andrew Wyeth. Used with permission.

06 05 04 03 02 01   10 9 8 7 6 5 4 3 2

A catalog record for this book is available from the British Library

Library of Congress Cataloging-in-Publication Data

Clement, Jane T., 1917-
  No one can stem the tide : selected poems, 1931–1991 / Jane Tyson
Clement.
     p. cm.
  ISBN 0-87486-900-5 (pbk. : alk. paper)
  I. Title.
  PS3553.L3933 N6 2000
  811'.54—dc21

                                                    00-010386

Printed in the USA

Contents

Foreword

JANE TYSON CLEMENT was born on October 1, 1917, on the Upper West Side of Manhattan. Though she lived there until she was nineteen (her father worked at Columbia University), she was never truly at home in the city but preferred Bay Head, New Jersey, where the family owned a summer house. Bay Head's windswept shore drew Jane back year after year; as she confided in her seventies, "There was something eternal about it that was always a rock and an anchor for me."

After graduating from the Horace Mann School in 1935, Jane went on to Smith College in Northampton, Massachusetts, where among other things she studied poetry under Grace Hazard Conkling. Scholar Howard Patch, whose lectures on Chaucer often digressed into conversations about faith, influenced her too. Jane left Smith in 1939 with a degree in English, but she felt her real education still lay ahead. Privately she yearned to move beyond the "frivolous, self-centered side of my nature...and to do something – anything – about the unfair treatment of workers, the hoarding of wealth in the hands of a few…and the prejudicial notion of the superiority of the white race."

Eventually this search led her to God, though first through disillusionment and confusion, and the frustrating recognition that the world's evil was as deeply embedded within organized Christianity as in secular life. Nevertheless, she found herself increasingly drawn into the quest for spiritual truth, particularly after reading the *Journal of George Fox,* which she discovered in a class on comparative religion: "Fox was a revelation to me, because I found I could respond to everything he believed and acted upon. And to think that there were still Quakers!"

World War II brought a series of teaching jobs in Pennsylvania, first at Germantown Friends, a private academy where she worked as an intern, and later at the Shippen School for Girls in Lancaster. It also brought marriage to Robert Allen Clement (the "R.A.C." to whom several poems in this collection are dedicated), a Quaker attorney and fellow pacifist.

In 1942 the Clements settled in Haddonfield, New Jersey. Bob practiced law in nearby Philadelphia, while Jane busied herself as a housewife and mother (they eventually had seven children) and did work for their local Friends Meeting, the Arch Street Yearly Meeting, and the American Friends Service Committee, a humanitarian organization. With one new responsibility after another, the demands on her time grew continually, and she began to feel pulled in all directions. Worse, she grew conscious of a nagging doubt that something about all her worthy activities was radically wrong: "Some subtle shift in base was necessary to jar the whole structure of my life into its God-given place."

In late 1952 the Clements came into contact with the Bruderhof ("place of brothers"), a Christian community movement with origins in Europe. Soon afterward they opened their home to itinerant members from the movement's South American base. Externally, the Bruderhof was a far cry from the Clements' milieu. Of one couple they hosted, Heinrich and Annemarie Arnold, Jane wrote, "They were obviously poor, obviously different as night and day from middle-class America…But their simplicity, warmth, naturalness, and self-effacement were like a refreshing wind." And their insistence on countering materialism and war not with words but by practicing voluntary community of goods offered a convincing – if unexpected – answer to her and Bob's growing frustration with the deadening complacency of post-war suburbia.

In late 1954 the Clements packed their belongings, put their house on the market, and moved to Woodcrest, the Bruderhof's new center in Rifton, New York. (They had already tested communal life during a visit to one of the group's South American settlements some months before.) They stayed for good. Jane explained:

> The undergirding facts were joy and love. And because of that we did not care how poor, how crowded, how (humanly speaking) precarious our situation, how much opposition we faced from family and friends, how physically tired we became, how sometimes we simply could not cope…Sometimes we were called upon to do the things we thought we were least fitted for, and discovered that by some power not of our making we *could* do them.
>
> We learned to trust, not merely in our human brothers and sisters, but in what had called us together and gathered us all out of our former ways, and in what lay behind and above and underneath everything: surrender and service to our Master, Jesus. His love upheld us…
>
> We were a small circle, from the most varied backgrounds and circumstances. Yet whenever we met, we felt something immediately – an inner

authority that did not come from the human individuals gathered there. We felt this inner security every day, in spite of all the uncertainties and unsolved situations; and this security did not come out of human confidence…

All of us who joined hands had dared something, had taken a leap into the unknown. How little we actually knew of what would be asked of us! How little we still know…

Though Jane never wavered in her dedication to the community she felt called to, she never stopped looking for a fuller, more genuine way to express her commitment. Practically, she found fulfillment in her work as a teacher at Bruderhof schools in New York, Pennsylvania, Connecticut, and England, where her passion for literature and history left its mark on an entire generation of students. In artistic terms, her seeking found an outlet in the never-ending search for a new image or an apt turn of phrase with which to capture a longing, a struggle, an illuminating moment.

It was not a self-important quest. As she wryly notes in one poem:

I stir no hands; I light no eyes from mine,
nor will my music ever shake the stars…

But in spite of such modesty, she could not escape her need to create – an urge so deep-seated and clear that she could assert:

> Oh, but I share the consciousness of breath;
> I have my purpose – I fulfill my days.
> Somewhere within me is the invulnerable flame
> which hissed and flared the day man first took fire…

There is nothing ostentatious about the poems in this book. In many, the word-pictures are drawn straight from the natural world: sunsets and surf, breaking ice, budding trees, and wheeling gulls.

Metaphors abound – the endless running of the tide a reminder of the endless cycle of life, the weathers of the heart mirroring the weathers of the sky – yet much of the verse works on an even simpler level: its sole purpose is praise. "Christ the Shepherd," for instance (a poem inspired by a trip through Wales), is first and foremost the outpouring of a devout heart.

Aside from *Strange Dominion,* a prize-winning narrative poem completed at Smith College in 1939, and *The Heavenly Garden,* a cycle printed by the Society of Friends in 1952, most of Jane's poems never traveled beyond the hands of her family while she was alive. She was less guarded with her plays and short stories, several of which appeared in *The Sparrow* (Plough, 1968, re-issued 2000 as *The Secret Flower*). Yet as one of her sons remarked after her death on March 21 of this year, his mother was so routinely dismissive of her gifts that he never even thought of her as a writer: "She certainly never seemed to think of herself in that way."

In a verse that laments the inadequacy of language to convey the stirrings of the soul, Jane writes:

> Words are the symbols of a mind's defeat,
> they shape the hollow air with transient life,
> and trick and twist; and make the spirit reel,
> vanish like ember's fire; devour and leave
> brave husks, and echoes of lost majesties.

Such ironic frustration is an inescapable part of practicing the writer's craft. But it is not the whole story. For if it is true (as it is often said) that a work of art bears the stamp of its creator, it must be that the creation of a poem involves the expenditure of love. And such love does have power, if only to alter the lens of the mind's eye and thus open it to new ways of seeing. Whether such claims can be made for the verses in this book, only the reader can decide.

C.M.Z.
July 2000

I

The Sea

1

The sea will follow me through all my years,
will lift my heart in song,
will quench my tears,
will lay benignant hands upon my head
at discontented whispers, sorrow led.
Death will find my body, hide it where
the ghastly shadows creep, all brown and sere;
will choke my singing voice,
will blind my eyes
to beauty which within the seasons lies,
the proofs of God, which fade and rise again,
restored by gentle fingers of His rain.
Yes, Death will find me.
Not immortal, I
who cling with earth-stained fingers
also die –
but not forever – no.
The sea will raise my song again,
remembering all my praise.

Gull, at the water's edge
mirrored in shining sand,
sleek in the silver wind
blown from the land;

in the clear fall of dark
past the thin pools of tide
with the gray sanderlings
swift at his side.

Outward beyond the eye
reaches the solitude
out to the end of time
where the winds brood.

One with his element,
quiet, unquestioning,
still, when the spill of wave
scurries the sanderling.

Dusk, and the spell of sea,
tide smell and all the vast
air for his wings when he
rises at last.

♦ THE SEA

MANASQUAN INLET I (1939)

Here to these rocks, not grown from the sand
of this shore, not spawn of this sea-edge,
the men have come, drawn by the storm wind,
the leap of spray, drawn by the sleek, deep
no-colored seethe of the water at evening,
drawn by the sure power of morning
down to this outpost, this strange ledge of life,
this channel of finite to infinite; here the men
gather; always their heads are turned seaward.
Between the great jetties of rocks the tides come
and roil and devour and are manacled.

Here the men sit, and watch the known water,
the known and familiar waters of inland;
river and cove where the heron has waded,
marsh where the kingfisher screamed his blue anger,
shallows and reedy lagoon where the huntsmen
have waited; these are the waters they know
and have lived from, these are the waters
that feed the great hunger of ocean;

now the need of the tide will carry them outward,
lost in the dark indefinable surge of the sea.

Watching the run of the tide, the dark river
of knowledge, outward to mystery, out
to be mingled and claimed, the men find a fragment
    of patience, a portion of fearlessness,
watching the waters go fearlessly outward to death.

MANASQUAN INLET II (1991)

No one can stem the tide; now watch it run
to meet the river pouring to the sea!
And in the meeting tumult what a play
of waves and twinkling water in the sun!

Ordained by powers beyond our ken,
beyond all wisdom, all our trickery,
immutable it comes, it sweeps, it ebbs
and clears the filthiness and froth of men.

5

Not now, but when it is too late for gladness
will we remember these days of sunlight
    and the clear water
netted with shadows moving and golden.
We will remember then, and the cry of the gull
will echo within us – gull's cry in the clean air.

There is no trace of an echo now – in these days –
for there is nothing here to send the cry back to us –
low water and high sky and the free air between –
Not now – but when it is too late for gladness.

THE INLAND HEART

The wind is singing on the sun-struck dunes;
eastward the wind blows, and the level sea
runs with shadows golden-green and dark;
and no gull cries nearby, but far away
where the black finger of the rocks is laid
the white wings flash, the voices flash, and far
across the moving stretch a white sail gleams.

Here I am lost, hedged in with hills and shade;
and the bright music ripples all day long —
thrush and vireo, and in the dark
the harsh cicada; and my soul must fail,
starve for the sudden, final thrust of sea
over the earth's curve, for the steady sun
that now the hills devour when day is done.

OCEAN

The birds that fly
in a shifting pattern
over the sea
with their eyes turned downwards —
what do they find
in the shining water?

Here on the shoal
the small waves crumble
bright in the sun
as the gull's swift pinion,
green and clear
in the depth of shadow.

Inland the osprey
bears its burden,
yield from the sea
out of these waters;
out of this field
a shining harvest.

SUMMER NIGHT STORM

The ranting of the gods, this tumbling sky,
this wind-strong rain which pelts against my cheek,
the world re-lit by lightning, and the lie
of tall sea grass low bent against the sand.

I stand here, strangely still, with all the world
tumultuous at my feet, and yet my heart
is stronger than the roaring wind that swirls
about my body, taut against its force;
that blows my eyelids shut, that locks my lips,
lest all my spirit end its restlessness
in one wild song.

9

BAY HEAD

This beach is the crumbled bone of many years;
who can construct again the skeleton
and join the scattered grains to their old form?

This sea is the blood and tears of all the ages;
who can define in it a single wound or grief —
so vast and mingled is the tide of pain?

Yet as the night floods darkness and the day
holds us in light, we walk earth's changing shore,
a brief path through the winds of good and evil,
    and of loneliness —

Therefore the sand and sea await us.

The inland is not safe from sea;
here where the meadows hold the day
and tongues are of the earth, the fields,
the sea-mind still is safe and free.

Perhaps it walks a little worn
between the elm and peakéd pine
or wakens restless to the sounds
of vigorous, healthy, country morn,

or finds the nights too long, too still,
lacking the rush and draw of wave,
or feels the eye cheated by the dark,
the sharp sky-crowding rise of hill.

But yet the wind of sea will run
the length of valleys and be here
sudden and full of space and wide
waters all leaping with the sun.

EBB TIDE

The tide will claim this shallow curve of sand
here where the thin waves curl and creep and die.
See – in this river no deeper than my hand
the young crab, pale and calico, slips by
into a safer, less tempestuous sea.
The eel, as silver and as quick as steel,
answers the sun; one moment he is free,
then the bird drops: a brief white circling wheel
cleaving the air, to splash, complete the arc;
the waters flicker, close, and leave no mark.

Take now this era, while the lengthening bars
stretch in the tawny shoals along the shore;
soon the sure rhythm of the moon and stars
will send the pliant waters in once more.

WINTER COAST

Gulls on the lonely beach
under the brooding sky;
over the darkened marsh
one gray gull's cry.

Wrack strewn upon the strand,
shards from the summer sea;
ripples from rising tide
creeping to me.

Winter is on the air,
sand drifted like the snow;
all the cold sky above,
sorrow below.

Boarded and silent wait
window and shuttered door.
Oh, will the summer joy
waken no more?

Summer of all mankind,
harvest from field and sea —
shattered and blown away —
no more to be?

Oh, but the promise lies
safe in His waiting hand;
sunrise again shall light
shimmering sand!

AT THE SHORE

Out of the black pool of sleep
the broken images like scattered sunlight
merge into morning, and I wake.

Here where the sea beats unangered
the gray gulls waddle along in the gray misty
morning
and rise on white wings over the white sea
transformed into grace in their own element.

Must we take lessons always from everything –
gulls fat and ridiculous dabbling their feet in the
tide-pool,
gulls flying sublime with the sunlight silver
upon them?

Better return to sleep and waken prosaic.
We were meant to both dabble and soar,
and even the loveliest wings get weary.

STALKING A GULL

With stealthy step they stalked the greedy gull.
A noose they laid around the tempting bread
and waited, breathless, while with stately tread
the old bird on the sand came closer. Wait!
Will he be fool enough to seize the bait?

Ah, clever bird! No boy bamboozles him —
he rises slightly and on fluttering wing
seizes the bread and veers off down the beach.
The sprung noose dangles empty. Out of reach
over the waves the sagacious seagull flies
with taunting laughter in his raucous cries.

II

Love and Longing

Now that my love has come I see the reason;
now I answer its demand;
it was here always just beyond my vision
waiting for your lifted hand.

It has the width of sea, the depth of shadow;
it holds the storm wind wild and strong,
and light drawn thin to stars in the sweep of heaven
and the prow's clear water-cleaving song.

My dear, I do not love you as you think,
not half in mirth, nor briefly, but forever.
Grant me some power to mend my imperfections;
admit me strength to make one long endeavor.

I am not all the surface gloss you think;
I have a deep glow, too, if you would see.
I would give proof of faith and fearlessness
if you would only care, and turn to me.

17

(TO R.A.C.)

The world will find me wiser and more kind
when you have gone; I've read my lesson well,
taking the best of you there was to learn,
seeing, though briefly, through your kindling eyes.

A child was fishing, and we stopped to see;
you climbed a cherry tree; we stayed beside
a colored beggar; and you showed me where
the periwinkle pushed up through the sod;
we watched one crooked moon break from the hills,
and saw a dark plane rise to merge with stars;
we talked until night turned around to light;
we laughed at nothing and at everything;
and when I sang somewhere within the house,
I stopped – to hear your music answering.

I cannot shut the door, and make an end,
and change into the old self: that would be
a true betrayal. It is best to take
all that you taught me, and to make it mine.

The world will find me wiser and more kind –
no brittle bitterness, no sterile hate
stays in these streets that you have walked of late.
I fear no evil, and my victory
gives me the lands wherein you made me free.

It is too late; you made me wait too long,
held my heart ringed with fire until the spell
broke and the flames were quieted to dust,
and I need wait no longer for your horn
sounding among the hills. I would be wise
to walk forgetting in this new release,
to give my free hands to this world's demand,
God's will – or the will of righteousness on earth –
too long was I apart from the needs of men,
single-starred and waiting, deep in sleep.

But lo, I rise and blow upon the ashes,
brush them aside, and seek the farthest hill,
calling your name and asking of your passage.
I am not free – I wait upon you still.

19

Now you are gone I shall not find delight
in dun soft hills at day's end, strong spring rain,
the deep and star-flecked sky of summer's night,
nor shall I feel the sharp, exquisite pain
of music reaching to immortal height
for beauty's truth. I shall not have again
the vigor of the ocean clear my sight
till nought but sky and sea and you remain.

Now you are gone, who lifted all my soul
to planes undreamt of. Beauty through your eyes
gave new enchantment to the years that roll
in terrifying silence. I was wise
beyond all men – but now that you have fled,
the magic which you gave to me is dead.

20

(TO ANNE)

When you died the wind died, too
and lay in the earth, grieving,
and over the earth the dusk came slow;
why did you think of leaving?

There was too little of your peace,
too little of your treasure;
we would be wise still if we judged
the wide hills by your measure.

For you the night is still;
the moonlight on the hill
shall come no more. And I
whose life was touched with flame,
if I stay not the same
because the flame must die,
you will not know.

For me the night will change,
the moonlight not be strange,
nor silvered hill. And you
whose life was turned to dark
sleep on and do not mark
if this small heart stay true,
if love will go.

It is for me to keep
the beauty, while you sleep
unsullied peace. And I
who cannot stay the years
nor live them all in tears
must watch the vision die
unchecked and slow.

22

The shadow on the grass,
the shadow thickens with the strength of sun,
    but sun will pass
into the monotone of mist and rain;
    the heavy leaf
hangs in the still wind, in the weight of sun;
    beyond belief
the days of rain, of blurred and mingled air.

But wait – remember!
There in the shadow of the leaf on grass –
    be still – remember.
The shadow is the symbol of the dark,
    the undefined;
I will be lost and merged and cold again,
    I will be blind
lacking your light, your positive demand
casting the shadows sharp on all my land.

23

We are tomorrow's past. O love, beware
lest lightly do we build what soon will fall,
and take too freely what is given us,
outstay our welcome with felicity,
and cast our doom on unsuspecting years.

Tomorrow this will be a yesterday;
a circle inwards from the outer tree,
a bit of rain that now has fed the flower.
Therefore, O love, beware lest lightly we
take our brief divinity and fail
and see no further than each other's eye
and then consume and turn to dust and die.

Between us lie the waters, dark and still;
for all our love, the sea will lie between;
for all our passion, which will surge and fill
the heart to breaking; and for all the clean-
stripped honest words of truth we speak;
still will those level depths, unchanged, serene,
deny us the last union which we seek;
and in the end we must accept despair,
knowing that what we breathe is mortal air.

O stars, yield me a portion of your still
vast reaches that the lovely wind has known;
O hall of night, where quiet walks in peace,
where bright flowers of a slumberous dark have grown,
speak to my heart of patience and release.
Single I stand upon the unsheltered hill.

If love will fail and all my faith must be
unbuttressed and unchampioned; if my soul
must hold itself its own security
and seek alone the hard and perilous goal,
give me – O earth that knows its destiny
unquestioning – the wisdom that the flower
finds when it dies, the knowledge that the hour
gains when the last clear minute ticks away;
yield me admittance, so with secret power,
though lone, I may go downward into day.

BIRDS IN THE ORCHARD

Now that it is over, I can see
why it has gone and why it could not last.
In autumn we can pick the laden tree
and know the purpose of the sunwild past.
Now that it is over, I have found
the twisted gourds, yellow along the vine;
the hard green apples scattered on the ground.
The clustered purple grapes, midwinter wine,
are sweet upon the air. This much I know:
as surely as the dusky plums will fall
our love was destined from the first to go.
Yet keep this trace of sweetness in the gall:
the waxwing and the oriole forgot
the ripened silver fruits that were our lot.

FRAGMENT

The lonely gull that beats with timeless wing
the timeless air over the ancient sea
is modern as the instant and the hour...

and so is love, that beats with timeless wing
upon the winds of hate, flies out the storm
and homes at last, inviolate to harm.

(TO R.A.C.)

I will remember you not as you are
but as I willed you were; and you shall move
soft as a shadow in my memory,
returning to the earth again at dark,
springing at sunrise to insistent life.

I will remember you not as you are;
your ghost that walks within my private heaven
will be a lie, and all your fellow-shades
that walk the sweet fields of my single past
shall be as wronged, as erred-upon, as you.

It is an odd thing how the heart is blind
and holds its self-deception like a gem,
an emerald, to gaze through at the world;
I will remember you; but you shall be
a bright-robed falsehood in my memory.

29

Remembering you, I have no other fear
than that you might forget and have no need
for further knowledge of my growing love;
all else is slight and dim – the broken world,
my soul's division, the uncertain year,
death of a season – these I come to dread
no more; it is your going that I wait,
taut and prepared to wrestle with despair.

Why do I fear? We have no vows to break;
we have our love between us and around
like a bright cloud of music, and the days
sing in their passage when I am with you.
If woe hides deep where joy has placed its claim
and sets the hour to strike across our name,
what use to break this sweet tranquility,
when you have turned to me, and I am you?

(TO R.A.C.)

The hedges blossom, and the night is sweet;
the field we walk in was this morning mown;
I watched them working in the steady sun;
I leaned against the fence and heard their talk
and heard the chipmunks squeak in fear of them.

Now it is darkness and the earth is still;
only the air breaks with the fireflies lights
that move like stars upon a sky of trees
so that the settled stars are pale beside
and the true heaven wan and far away.

Tell me the farther sky demands our eyes;
tell me the morning is in store for us
and that we travel through this instant's peace
into the burning sun; could I forget?
Life's life, and this sweet interval no less

than the hard duty and the twisted hand.
Take no guilt upon you for this hour;
if we are circled by infinity,

made great by fading past the bitter earth,
it is our right, the right of breath and bone,

and as betrayal lies within our kiss,
and no forsaking; need we look on joy
as guilt, take grief as duty, and deny
this hour of darkness, deep and double-starred?
Now in the field, the scattered grasses lie

where the men labored in the steady sun,
and the lights flicker in the bordering trees.
The hedges blossom and the night is sweet;
over the earth the winds of slumber run;
I see the shadows of our two hands meet.

31

It's not what happens that decides our end;
it's how the heart takes hold of it and makes
an open wound of pain, or wisdom's scar.
What my heart makes of this, the days will tell.
Therefore return in some safe-distanced year

    to see if I am invalid and lame
or scarred but otherwise quite wise and well.
But do not look to find me quite the same.

(T O R . A . C .)

One who has loved is never quite alone,
though all the hills declare our solitude.
Having known you, I am no more afraid,
the essential singleness of blood and bone
when dispossessed, comes never in return;
one who has loved is never quite alone.

33

(TO R.A.C.)

I do not swear I will remember you;
I have sworn that before – and have forgot,
and vowed eternities too many times
to tarnish this with phrases I hold cheap.
I will not even say you are my love;
the word is trite, beribboned, tired with use,
and has grown sickly with the world's abuse.

I say that you are young, when all around
the years are weary, hearts destroy themselves,
and the bright morning of an April day
scarcely moves the dark; and you are clean
when dust of ages blows about the fields
and the new corn is stifled at its birth.
I say that I would choose, if choice were mine,
with all the honesty my heart can give,
to be your fellow out across the hills.

I do not swear I will remember you.
The lines we follow may diverge today
to meet each separate end. But I can say
when I am old, that once the world was true
and I was fearless and was not alone,
and broke the barriers of blood and bone
into the regions of a brighter star;
and when I smell the fragrant dusk of spring
I will be still with joy, remembering
these days no threat, no falsity can mar.

34

(T O   R . A . C .)

Look, my love, the mist is on the fields
and westward where the wooded slopes are dark
one star is steadying the falling night;
this is the last hour for the distant thrush;
listen, a church bell tolls beyond the hill:
the valley holds the tokens of the day —
nine strokes — and slowly lets them drift away.
Then thrush and bell and all the trees are still.

Now will you turn and let me speak with you?
What will bear witness to my steadfast love?
How can I say it, show it, make it sure,
then set it free to journey through the world?
I give it up; it would take forever after
to prove in words what only life can show,
and there is too much need of present laughter,
and, in the end, I know that you will know.

LOVE IS THE LAW OF LIFE

Am I deceived, if I have given love
the voice to spell the essence of my days,
authority to rule in all its ways
and with its urgency my spirit move?
Am I betrayed, in yielding love this power,
in giving it the scepter and the crown,
the brightest banner and the sole renown,
unchallenged victor over every hour?

    It is not I but love who is deceived,
    and love who risks disaster, trusting me,
    and puts its energy in jeopardy
    and will by my defaulting be bereaved.

I have not strength nor majesty to bring
sufficient zeal to such a lord and king.

It is a long dream that threatens us.
Not tomorrow – not for many morrows –
may we waken; and who's to say if ever
we will find the earth real under our hands again,
and these days live and quick, a pulse in the wrist.
(Now I waken early, in the silver of November,
in the pale dusk of morning; down the street
a wagon creaks; a man whistles;
    a few leaves scrape and rustle;
then I sleep again, knowing I will wake again,
    in spite of dreaming.)

But the long dream, waiting in mist –
when will it cover us; when will the deep wave
sweep in and cover us? And when will we rise
out of the deep shadows upward, upward to sunlight
    and air and the sound of voices
speaking our names in love and brotherhood?
Fearless we must be, and sure, though worlds merge
    and tremble.
(Now a man whistles and kicks through the leaves;
my window is pale in the dusk of morning;
I turn back to sleep, but I will wake again, after.)

APRIL

The buds unfold upon the bough
that slept the bitter winter through.
Whose voice has bid them waken now?
The voice that also spoke to you.

The flowers stir with April rain;
they thrive and grow and blossom free.
Whose voice has bid them rise again?
The voice that also spoke to me.

The birds are here that once had flown
the hidden highways of the sky.
We know – we know who called them home,
for we have heard Him, you and I.

TO MY UNBORN CHILD

I carry life or death within me;
this little stirring, blind and pushing creature
is the sweet paradox
    inevitable
weighing me down with either joy
    or sorrow.

Teach me, my little one, the slow acceptance,
whether death or life is borne within me.

I am in God's hands, and you
in God's hands
    through me –
all of it God's: the light, the dark,
    the winter,
and this wild, petal-drifting,
    sun-dazed May.

39

Child, though I take your hand
and walk in the snow;
though we follow the track of the mouse together,
though we try to unlock together the mystery
of the printed word, and slowly discover
why two and three make five
always, in an uncertain world –

child, though I am meant to teach you much,
what is it, in the end,
except that together we are
meant to be children
of the same Father
and I must unlearn
all the adult structure
and the cumbering years

and you must teach me
to look at the earth and the heaven
with your fresh wonder.

THE CHILDREN

They are not mine, they are not really mine,
not even in the night when they cry out,
and I, half-stifled with the need of sleep,
stumble awake and go to quiet them.

Not by my grace or genius have they grown,
nor by my merit did I bring them forth,
nor by that sealed and deep-loved partnership;
the light that crowns them is none of my own.

And in my tempers and my discontents
when my own devil mutters and is bad,
I must remember still they are not mine,
not even to deny – but wholly thine.

Into the dark which is not dark
but only the light we cannot see,
reluctantly I let you go.
What was your source – children of years?
Surely I cannot claim your birth;
for when I found you, even then
you were not strangers to the earth.

I was the privileged, to disclose
briefly, a portion of your days.
Now you are free – but not complete;
for none of us is this the end.
Somewhere the valley holds the mist,
the four fields shimmer in the haze,
the man of patience and the child
and the sea-eyed girl draw deep their breath
and live, and have no fear of death.

VIGIL

Sometimes I have sat alone in the tall grass
    by the side of the path
and watched the edge of the woods,
there, right there, where the witch hazel grows,
and the dogwood and the elder bushes,
and wondered and waited.

What would I do, O Master,
    if you came slowly out of the woods.
Would I know your step?
Would I know by my beating heart?
Would I know by your eyes?
Would I feel on my shoulders, too,
    the burden you carry?
Would I rise and stand till you drew near
    or cover my eyes for shame?

Or would I simply forget everything
except that you had come and were here?

Today you have not come, not this way.
But that you are somewhere,
	of that I am sure,
and we must, each one,
have your welcome waiting.

ENTREATY

Over the fields and the woodland road
the killdeer are crying, my own dear heart.
Over the meadows the larks call home,
my voice is seeking for you alone.
Say – will you come?

Where the stream ripples, the red-wing sings;
the crows fly down to the stubble corn;
the alders are thick with catkin and cone.
See – are you watching the cloud-strewn sky
as the south winds blow?

Over the pasture the plovers cry;
the fringe of the wood is alive with song,
and the white sheep crop in the wakening green.
The Shepherd stands by the pasture bar –
let us take Him our lambs.

III

Art

44

"I AM NO ARTIST..."

(No true desire burns within me now.
I am no artist, lonely and supreme,
fulfilled within myself, needing no hand
to touch, no eyes to smile, no lips to speak.)

The wind roars in the pines and I am sad,
wanting your presence here. The bluejay flies
over the ruffling water to the hill,
lonely and dark and scattered yet with leaves.
I'd ask you why this bird will never go
south when the prophesying geese honk past
into a sunny heaven. Why stay here
where snow blinds and the icy dawn is still,
when there are strong blue wings to bear you out
into a wide sky, into a singing land?
I'd ask you that and wait for your reply,
knowing your wisdom must exceed my own.

(The wind roars in the pines and I am sad,
wanting you here beside me. Now I know
I am no artist, lonely and supreme,
needing no hand to touch, no eyes to smile.
Only your lips, your presence here, would seem
to send me winging southward mile on mile.)

TO ARCHIBALD MACLEISH

I touched his hand, but he will not remember.

I looked into his eyes, tea-colored,
and he smiled at me,
not knowing who I was or caring
other than that I was young and just beginning.
He did not know that I stood then
where he once stood,
or that I wanted what he now had found;
will and power of words.
He lays his thoughts
clearly like jewels flashing in the light,
simple, unset except with what the mind
must have to shape itself.

I touched his hand, but he will not remember.

I aim to be a poet. That I have over him.
I aim at what he is. The fight is mine.
He looked as though he knew once what it meant
and had not quite forgotten.

I touched his hand, but he will not remember.

WORDS

I feel the stirring of the unprofitable years,
the weight of prophecy and ancient grief.
We talk, the words flash golden and then die;
the thin smoke curls, beyond the window's dark
a bat cheeps, faint, repeating, in the night.

Words are the symbols of a mind's defeat,
they shape the hollow air with transient life,
and trick and twist and make the spirit reel,
vanish like ember's fire, devour and leave
brave husks and echoes of lost majesties.

MUSIC

Try to define it, seek in vain its source
or where it vanishes. By formulas
and theories tell me what it is I breathe,
what makes the stars bright, why the waves are long
unending servants of a master-moon.
Tell me why I love, why I see blue
in a sky where no blue is, but only light.
Tell me my pen is nothing but a force
my hand (which is not either) works upon,
and that the keys my fingers linger on
are never ivory, but are molecules
"gyrating in a predetermined form."
Tell me the scent of lilacs is not real
but only a fusion working on my sense.
Tell me the fresh green of a new spring lawn
is chlorophyll. Tell me turgidity
makes hyacinths stand stiff beside the path.

Tell me all this. I shall believe you true
and grant you what you say. But music – there
try to define it! Seek in vain its source,
its essence, where it waits for my two hands
to call it forth from yellowed, singing keys.
Put it in tubes, solve its complexities,
tell what its structure is – yes, if God will.
But you can hound it down the path of years
and curse and stamp. It shall elude you still.

WRITER'S (ABDOMINAL) CRAMP

Maybe Milton tired of his own words
and Keats' own beaded bubbles wearied him,
and Shakespeare's phrases to his ears were bleak,
sounded and resounded from the boards.

How it would comfort me to know they felt
a little nauseated now and then
with their own fare; for I have grown quite ill
with eating of the food my pen does grill.

SALEHURST BELLS

Above: the tumult of the bells;
beneath: the dark, still church
crouched in its ancient mysteries;
between: the ringers' toil.

Men with stalwart skill now grasp the ropes;
eyes flick to eyes, sure pattern in the mind,
and in the hidden chamber overhead
the bells leap to obey; the treble hunts its way
amid the throng of clamorous voices
and finds home:

cry joy, cry grief – cry birth, cry death
cry years, cry pain – cry war, cry peace
cry faith, cry truth – cry dawn, cry dark

while in the dusky night the valley lies
and listens, and remembers all;
the brooklet murmurs in its bed:
"Nothing is lost; no passing tone is dead."

THE ORGAN AT VESPERS

From what depth of power do you arise
to sweep across the tired hearts of these
small earth-bound people? You have closed their eyes,
and locked their lips. You have kept their minds
only to do your will, to reach the last
clear pinnacle of beauty through your sound.
Great mellow climbing chords, within your realm
intangible to mortals, yet long sought
by those aspiring to a perfect thought,
what limit has God set that you can touch
only so far our consciousness with light
from that strange truth which shines across our days?

The flood of sound flows back into the dark.
I stir and rise, remembering only then
the gods of music are the hands of men.

BACH INVENTION

If I could live as finished as this phrase,
no note too strong; each cadence purposed, clear,
the logic of the changing harmony
building and breaking to a major chord
strangely at home within a minor web
of music; if I could define my end,
from the beginning measures trace my course,
I might be old and prudent, shown by laws
how to devise a pattern for my days
and still be free, unhampered, yet refined.

He sat before the keys and turned the notes
into a fabric of design and peace;
here are the notes, the keys, my fingers free
to run them through their course, and here my mind
seeing his wisdom work within the chords,
finding his knowledge in the finished line.
I would be wise if such restraint were mine.

BRAHMS

If I once knew of sorrow it has gone.
Gladness alike has vanished in the light.
Music alone remains. Some wandering song
struck his quick heart – struck, and with the might
God-given, of harmony, he plays it out,
drives it through until the very end,
catches what with lonely words I sought,
seals up the wounds that I with words would mend.

Measureless, weightless, sightless power of notes,
filling my vision, filling all my life,
intermedium of these dull motes
that ever are within my heart at strife,
revealer of what our eyes could never see,
you and eternity alone are free.

DARK INTERVAL

You were a music once, beyond my fingers,
beyond the keys man makes and plays upon;
the sweet chorale is finished and is ended;
the harmony has risen and has gone
into the mind of God where it will linger
always among all beauty we have lost.
Here there is silence sudden and profound;
here I call out: the hollow echo answers;
no cool thrush speaks of evening from the thickets
within the white drugged tautness of the noon;
there is no upward rush of your bright song:
only this lack of melody, this deep,
dark interval too empty and too long.

Only the past will yield to poetry;
only the lost years that the wind blows back
out of the stars to mingle with our breath,
so that our tissues take them in again
until they surge once more in human veins
and beat behind our eyes, and know no death.

The present has a substance solid, gross —
clay to be molded, granite to be struck,
passion to flare, and timber piled to burn;
the past is our music, our essential air,
earth of our spirit, deep sea of our mind,
and out of its return we know, we learn.

ON BEING STIRRED
BY AN APRIL SHOWER

A new poem, a new shape,
an ancient thought
now freshly caught
and taught
to rhyme...

Why take the time?
Why not live and let
    the moment live?
Why should I give
effort and pain
when April rain
heedless,
    lovely,
        necessary,
is needless of me
or my music?

IV

Nature

FIRST SNOW

I felt it coming in the thin, blue air.
I saw it in the sky, delaying there,
divinely punctual, for the secret nod
and signal for descent from some snow-god.

I should have known the clouds would waver down
slowly, until they lay upon the ground
and we could walk, feet kicking up the sky
beneath, that once was hanging white and high.

I should have been prepared for this new sight
of something moving downward in the night,
of snow-flame creeping outward on the trees,
and gathering on the roofs, along the eaves,

ticking against the window, flickering by,
or landing on the ledge to melt and die,
holding its pattern for one little space
of time against the wood like fragile lace.

I covered up the flower beds to prepare
for what I knew was near, yet unaware
I let the white drift downward in the still
cold air, to find defeat upon my sill.

CARDINAL

The tides of winter now are running strong,
high on the shores of every day they flow
piling the meadows with vast waves of snow,
stifling to whispered silk the river's song.

The tides of winter and the tides of spring –
the wild abundance of a summer's day –
autumn's ingathering! Time will never stay.
In the bare maple, hear the cardinal sing.

A CRICKET IN WINTER

Thin voice of summer;
faint memory:

hardhack and meadowsweet
near the berry patch,
and on the far edge of wood
a small bird dropping to the meadow grass;
the August sun, yellow and sweet,
and all around us the rustle
    of cricket.

Now the cloak of snow lies
everywhere, and the quiet trees
stand deep in their memories;

and within by the warmth,
under the books, somewhere,
now here, now there, this thin
chant, cheerful, undaunted,

and I smell the wild
bergamot again.

THE RABBIT

He hops and thinks awhile and hops again,
then rubs his ear with one curled-over paw;
up in the empty tree the black crow crouches,
darkens the frosty silence with his caw,
ruffles and stirs and wings across the field;
the rabbit does not move, but meditates,
not bothering to turn his thoughts to me.

I hold his small indifference like a shield
over my heart; there are too many eyes
which care to see just for the sake of seeing
and are not swift to help, and are not wise.

DUSK

In the winter dusk a cardinal is the last to come,
a cardinal and sometimes the song sparrow.
The cardinal glows like a coal in the gathering dark
and I am sad if I know the food is gone —
for if I go out with more, he will fly away
    and not return,
not knowing my intentions.

Tonight the moon is rising through the spruce.
Over the road, in the Yale woods, they have been
    lumbering,
cutting down in a day what it took weeks to fell
    in the old time,
        not long ago at that.

Where will the birds shelter, and the deer?
When will such trees grow back, in what new day?

WINTER

The dark emerging trees
from the new-winter wood
are lovelier than leaves,
as cold is also good.

The heart's necessities
include the interlude
of frost-constricted peace
on which the sun can brood.

The strong and caustic air
that strikes us to the bone
blows till we see again
the weathered shape of home.

No season of the soul
strips clear the face of God
save cold and frozen wind
upon the frozen sod.

FEBRUARY THAW

On the wet bank's rim we stand,
the air wild with the beating rain;
the sodden wood beyond awry
with wild wind from the driven sky:
    (and I know deeply and with pain
    we stand here once and not again.)

The crumbling, heaving thrust of ice,
the thundering tumult of the falls,
familiar crisis of the year,
the swift blood beating in the ear:
    (but only once, within the heart
    the ice piles ready to depart.)

The men are knotted by the dam,
the grinding floes rear up and roar
and press and push; and with a shout
we watch the jam come tumbling out:
    (so may we shout, so may we sing,
    O blessed thaw, O holy spring.)

MAGNOLIA

It has two falls; once when the flowers are sweet
past bearing, and drift down to touch the grass,
circling around like a sinking dancer's skirts.
(Who gathers the fallen petals in the night?
who takes the magic of the tree away,
leaving it green and plain, bereft of bees,
and of its scent, which held the birds bewitched?)

It has two falls; again when the maples flame
and scatter gold across the tarnished grass,
it lets its ordinary mantle drop
unnoticed, and the silver limbs are bare.

It is at peace now when the silence holds
the winter hillside, now the cheeping bat
hangs shut-eyed in his cave, the birds are gone
save for the sparrows scuffling in the snow
and the shrike that watches from the thorny hedge.

It is a tree of sorrow, for its hour
Of greatest beauty is its earliest.
It has no last triumphant blaze of light
to dream of in the long, snow-silenced night.

PETER'S SONG

Down near the brook the grass is wet
and the flags are rustling stiff and blue;
the cress is fresh where the water runs
over the stones and the willow roots.

(There was a girl I showed this to;
she asked me whether the flags were blue
even in winter. I gave her cress
to eat, and she liked the bitterness.)

Up in the orchard the apples lie
scattered around in the rippling grass.
Off in the distance the hills are dark
and the fences wind like ivory snakes.

(There was a girl I showed this to;
she asked if the hills were ever blue
as the waves. She said that the shining stones
were white in the sun like pirate bones.)

The thrushes sing in the shadowed woods
and the whippoorwills in the scented dark.
(But there is a girl with the sea in her eyes
who never has found where the mayflower lies.)

THE MEADOW

The meadow grows
thinking itself as safe, as far, as untouchable
as the stars it stares at on clear nights;
and the rabbits grow numerous in the thick grass
and the flowers come up heedlessly;
the larks whistle to the morning
and come back sure and steady as the dusk
    to their nests;
the ants crawl up the grass stems to balance,
moving their feelers, and retire,
a little heady with glimpse of space and sun,
    but still contented,
to their realm of tall stem, tall shadows, dirt,
    and long cool aisles of roots.

Well – there will come the hay harvest.
We are not the only ones to hear the sough
    and fall of our safe domains;

we know the threat, the sure intrusion;
therefore I stand and watch as the meadow
    meets its destiny;
and I feel my own earth tremble,
    my own heart perish.

NIGHT RAIN

The drenched smell of wet earth,
the black road shining,
the light in the window
sending a white shaft
through the mist.

The drowsy sound of wind
moiling in the trees.

And far away the sky
like a cave of light
over the town,
far away but there
like a great furnace.

MIDSUMMER DAY SKETCHES

I

At the edge
I stand here by the hawthorn tree
deep in the English meadow grass
to watch the wheeling swallows pass
over the green waves of the grain
beyond the hedge.

II

The waves of grass under the wind
all run uphill, endlessly,
grass pouring uphill all the sunny afternoon,
with shadows sailing dark, over a tawny sea.

AUTUMN

The passing of the summer fills again
my heart with strange sweet sorrow, and I find
the very moments precious in my palm.

Each dawn I did not see, each night the stars
in spangled pattern shone, unknown to me,
are counted out against me by my God,
who charges me to see all lovely things:
the clear, unresting moon, the night-filled sea,
rolling shadowed waves along the shore,
the cool wind, speaking softly of the flowers
in moon-drenched beauty by the garden wall,
the bright, relentless glamor of the day,
the ocean, curling out upon the sand,
and tumbling foamy combers to their end.

Each time my eyes uncomprehending saw
these lovely things, and passed them by unmoved,
the keen-eyed angel, frowning, moves the pen
and leaves his record stained, immutable.

HARVEST DUSK

The sheep crop on the stony hill,
the martins skim the evening sky,
the golden day-fall lingers still;
one star stands high.

The barley field is silver-gold;
it stirs beneath the breath of night.
The thrushes pour their songs of old
in fading light.

Thy harvest yield is ever free,
so let it grow within my heart
to bring me into peace with thee,
no more apart.

NOVEMBER RAIN

Now we must look about us. Near at hand
cloud like a fist has closed on all the hills
and by this meager daylight on our land
we see just this, and this, and not beyond.

The sodden trees emerge and stand revealed;
we must acknowledge each one as it is,
stripped and stark, its basic structure clear,
the last leaves fallen, summer's season dead.

And day on day the soft mist softly falls
as the long rain drives across the field
and all the while what we had seen beyond
is lost and shut as if it never were.

And we look closely at each other now,
the bleak roots, black grass, and the muddy road,
the litter that we never cleared away,
the broken flowers from a summer's day —

Oh, stark and clearly we must look within
to weigh at last our purity and sin.

Oh, lovely hills in sunlight far away,
Oh, curving valley where the river sings!
Remembering, we live this discipline,
and hope still beats about us with strong wings.

SUSSEX DECEMBER

The valley hangs in misty rose,
the trees lace black against the sky,
the brief day drowses to a close
and all the birds are still.

But sudden in the West a fire,
under the trees a springing flame,
light level blazing past until
the sun drowns in the hills.

ROOKS

There is a tumult in the skies;
over the cedar rooks now thresh and rise
to fill the wild wind with their cries.

Their fathers had a freehold here.
Before the Romans marched up from the shore
they set their seal upon the year
with tumbled nests and raucous arguments.

The Great Storm could not drive away
their claim upon the ancestral place,
their fealty, their right to stay,
these fields their own, this sky
their old accustomed space.

The earth's good, in spite of evil;
     the earth's good; I've tasted it,
tasted water sweet out of the rock's side
and the darkness, pressed with my fingers
the furry leaves till the scent lingered,
run over the dunes seaward with the wind
fighting me, lain in the hollows soft
with fern and sharp with ground pine
with the sky cupped over me
     and a few clouds moving;
followed the thrush into the thicket at evening,
where no star scattered the dark
of wind in the leaves; plunged into the green water
down to the furrowed sea floor
where there is silence and slow light
and the feel of sand to pushing fingers,
and the pound of blood against weight
     and alien element.

Who's to say whether the words of one faith
     can hold off destruction?
I say the earth's good – does that make it so?

What is the earth then — what we have made of it?
Is the earth us in our passage? What after us?
Tide and the wheel of time, and the air turning?
No longer the stir of light under the poplars,
or the red-eyed moth that clings to the lamp-pull
    and looks at me?

Earth's good, as I've known it; I for one
will cry yea from the street corners, will sing
    for the hills to echo,
will take pain and fire and love's passing
    as part, not judgment;
the heart must have both to be whole,
    must know fear to be brave;
laughter chokes unless there are tears before
    and tears after.

Earth's good, as I've seen it,
    and I've seen a little;
held a young squirrel in my hand, at least,
    with his teeth in my finger,
watched morning come out of the sea,
    and the dark settle.

SWALLOWS

The swallows come rollicking down the evening sky,
up our valley north in a scatter they fly,
swoop to the meadow, then veer to cover the pond,
hover and droop, then up and away and beyond!

Were I sky-born, not a human child,
I'd be a swallow, too – light, free and wild,
cleaving the evening sky with unerring wing,
praising God in my flight – no need to sing.

RAINBOW

The silly sheep
busy at the wet grass in the sparkling morning
never know, as the fine rain drifts down,
that from their meadow now a rainbow springs.

I and the chaffinch,
by the ancient oak,
look and look as the mystic colors glow,
and the silly sheep
munching at their meadow
never know
the glory resting
upon their woolly backs.

OLIVER

He lies among the lilies
under the tall leaves
where the earth is cool.

With pale green eyes
he surveys
the dazzle of the noonday,
the passage of a cabbage butterfly,
the dart of a humming bird,
the ravaging bee,
the whirr of sparrow wing.

He lies under the cool leaves
until he hears my step up the path.
Then he may rise, if he chooses, to greet me,
as he may blink in the sudden sun
when I part his cover,
and look away as if to say,
"I have too much to attend to.
Later please, not now."

Oliver was the writer's cat

EVENING

A sunset meadow in the sky,
the cloudy sheep are drifting by
into the quiet fold of night —
cloud sheep of a nursery rhyme
from a lost and purer time.

STORM

When the lions of the sky are roaring,
when wind-eagles high above are soaring,
black horses of the West are thundering on,
and rain like stinging bees is pelting down,

run to the hedges – come – and hide with me.
There we can watch the fury, feel the beat
of some wild weather-anger at our feet
and crouch like frightened rabbit in its form
to wait, unseen, the passing of the storm.

How can we hear
the sound of wind
within the rain,
though wind is still?
How can we see
the look of dusk
upon the hill,
though it be day?

Rain is not rain
alone; nor day
completely day;
nor is the earth
solely of earth —
and in the mind
one finds the heart —
and in the seed
death holds a part.

BUTTERFLY BALLET

Along the ragged edge of dune
he swooped, he leapt, he twirled, he spun,
he swept his net with antic grace,
a fierce expression on his face.

And as we watched upon the beach
he stalked his foe just past his reach,
then lunged, then ran, then lunged once more –
and fell exhausted on the shore.

But ah! Here comes another! See,
drifting southward waveringly.
Up, up, oh dancer! One more try!

With trembling knees he starts to rise;
his sly, approaching foe he spies;
he waits, he lurks, he leaps, he spins,
he twirls his net, he halts, he grins.
He shouts then to the autumn sky
with a vast triumphant cry!
What has he caught?…a butterfly.

BOULDER

This boulder is no monument to war
(no names, no dates, no honorable words),
it hunches on the hill, half hid in ferns,
above our glacial meadow flat and rich,
and watches our frail doings year by year.

This is no monolith that man has raised;
no nameless human toil has placed it here —
but the dispassionate and grinding ice,
age upon voiceless age, and now it lies,
mute witness to Earth's passage through the skies.

MOON

Earth's shadow is over her;
far in the western fields,
see – where the stars are few,
where the light scatters,
where the clear wind will rise
upward across the land –
there is the silver horn
curled on the sky.

The shadow is over her,
flung from this meager star;
somewhere she shines complete,
marred by no drift of dark;
tranquil she takes her light
from the abundant sun.
Mirror of fire – oh pale
passionless wanderer!

THE BRASS LOCUST

So now again the tide wanes and the air
is rich with what would rather be forgotten;
and hard on the moving, on the changing wind
the eternal locust sounds its sharp despair:

the rasp of autumn and the rasp of heat,
metal of prophecy but not of peace,
awl in the ear to make us bondsmen here,
brand in the flesh of mind; under the beat

of sun, of light rain, of the dazzling earth
we lose the visioned, the encompassing eye;
the brass of locust boring in the noon
speaks for the alien and the coming dearth:

the unwise lift their heads, remembering cold,
regathering wisdom, as the sun grows old.

Now the westering sun swings down,
blazing into the hills of home
in rim of fire and golden sky,
it ends its circle and is gone

and all the little stars wink on;
the small heart waits for sleep,

and when the new-made morning breaks,
it is the sun that summons us,
springing out of the eastern edge,
spilling warmth upon the land,
soaring in measured, ancient course;
the small heart labors on.

Candlelight, to those who know no other,
has every element of energy
and set in myriads on brave candelabra
will grace with splendor the bright halls of kings
and gleam and flash from every flickering mirror
 and in its single gleam
 a simple stalwart beam
can hold the shadows back and light a room
with faces, hands, and all the stuff of life
caught in the warmth of living candlelight.

Though man's invention should make obsolete
the tallow and the wick, the hanging molds,
and night be driven back by manmade moons,
this little flame, this day, will be sufficient,
will be enough to those who know no other
and light the deathbed and the low-hung cradle,
alike the face of friend, the face of lover.

LANDSCAPE
WITH LAPACHO TREE

Where is home?

Where willows gather
on the crumbling banks
and water rustles in the roots
and swallows skim;
the elm up-rushing
flings its falling green;
the still pine stands against the West.

Home is not only these.

The pink cloud of the flowering tree
across the camp
far, in the ridge of woods
struck by the dying sunlight
the lapacho,
and the river parrots
slowly flying
like herons.

Neither is strange,
      not now,
when the heart has followed
the curve of the world
to find the same welcome.

GRAY FOXES

The foxes come at twilight when the birds are still,
the small gray foxes fleet of foot and wise.
Out of the bracken and the fringe of darkness
    they appear.
The glow of torchlight shows their emerald eyes.

The coons that lumber from the brush come later
    in the dark,
and in our lantern light their eyes are gold.
They are the midnight prowlers and the vandals
    of the night,
leaving their wreckage, mischievous and bold.

But, oh, the nimble foxes are so fleet of foot
    and neat,
they float like moving shadows from the wood.
I whistle, and they stop, ears poised, and turn
    their heads
to me with eyes alight, as if they understood.

Fern fiddleheads
like a loved story
whose ending we know well
and wait for —

EVENING AT DARVELL

The sleepy droning of late rooks in the trees
and one plane homing over very high
winking red and green, with steady stars
already lighted in the skies.

The world in tumult, far away, of no account
the terror and the anguish unredeemed,
black against the peace that God would give,
against the space of Heaven and purity.

Time and Change

SONNET

Seeking the fact that lies behind the flower
the soul will break its own mortality;
searching the time that lies beyond the hour
the soul will yield its blind serenity;
that is but briefly to be ill at ease
and then forever to be tranquil-eyed,
stirring the wrath of temporal deities
who hurl pale lightning when they are defied.
The least fine sheaf of millet will repay
the soul's slow contemplation, and the still
ages of starlight between day and day;
the climb is steep to mount a sudden hill;
but if man, fearless, follows stars, he'll find –
lo, he is more than stars, and more than mind.

(TO R.A.C.)

The days that are vanished return to me now,
and the old gods, whose fires are dead,
their dust kindles, and the old dirges
sound in the temples; and over valleys
the last birds fly seaward with strange wings
that have not beaten the air since the first forests
crumbled; and flowers of long-forgotten woodlands
rise again, and voices stir in the hills.

I can remember now the beginning of all things;
I can feel the first footfall on solid earth,
touch the first flower that opened to sunlight –
pale-green, speckled, with three leaves, nameless –
and the first laughter echoes again, and the first singing.

The days that are vanished return to me now;
now there is lost to me nothing of what has been,
even the old mountains that sank into the sea,
or the least stalk of crabgrass, three-pronged and dusty.

SEA ECHO

If at this juncture I am pressed with sharp
remembering, with the weight of other days,
of sea mist, of the rustling early grass
where little sparrows forage; and the sand
blown in long streamers on the empty road
speaks to me suddenly of other Junes;
and the slow osprey winging out to sea
transports me to that lost shore instantly;
if I am vulnerable to this extent
in these the middle years, with more ahead
presumably than that which lies behind,
how shall I bear the past when I am old?

To garner wisdom is to lose regret;
if that is true I am not wise at all,
standing here weeping for a happy youth,
puzzling over what the past becomes
seen through the lenses of the gathering years.

I must become accustomed to return,
altered myself, to the unaltered scene.
Then if the heart accepts the happiness
of now, not longing for the what-has-been,
the sweet sea echo will not mock, but bless.

93

(T O R . A . C .)

Will there be a cold sky over us, ice in the wind,
a dead earth under our feet, and our hands parted?
We who have walked in the mist of a new morning,
what will time do to us, what will be proven of length
    as the days gather?

Have you a fear of it? Not I — not ever —
when the oak holds fewer leaves of a last summer
I shall not mind, having you; when the last asters go
there will be flowers waiting under the snow
    for a new season.

And, as I know now, I shall know then in a surer fashion
the deep valleys of your heart and the bright mountains;
though I have heard the cynic, I shall believe the faithful.
Fear's roots cannot live in the deep earth we have found,
    where evil withers.

ANCESTOR

The sound of ax upon tree
in the deep wood
is a sound not known to me,
nor the song of the well-rope
as the bucket dips,
swallows its burden,
and rises again;
nor the creak of the fire crane
as it swings the kettle
over the blaze;
nor the steady, muffled plod
of the plow horse.

But the oriole's bright, tentative
whistle in the treetops,
the wren in the apple tree
spilling its blossoming notes,
the shrill rooster piercing
the morning with assurance,
the sleepy whirr of bees among the lilacs –
these I can share with you.

WINDOVER HILL

Bird in the hedge
and ancient tree,
out of the past
now answer me,

gull on the meadow,
wind from the sea
blown from the ages
wild and free:

here on this hillside
who has stood
watching the smoke rise
out of the wood,

watching the marshes
misty and blue,
and the lane rimmed
with hawthorn and yew?

Out of the earth
both flint and grain;
out of the heaven
sun and rain;

are we not brothers
now – and then –
with the same Master
for all men?

FOREBODING

Across the shallows tawny shadows run
and one grey osprey circles in the sun
over the still, green sea. The moment rests
hot on the sands and on the sunwhite dunes;
the moment is perfection, with the slow
draw of the waves, the gliding of the bird
lonely and silent in the empty air.

It will not last: the osprey will wing off
into the West, the tide will turn, the sky
pile up the clouds, the great grey shadows run
across the sands and shut away the sun.

LANDING AT DELOS

The ships drawn up along this lonely shore,
the flickering fires and voices tinged with grief,
dull with discouragement, worn-out with life,
what quiet, tragic witness do they bear
to death and hate and wearied women's tears!
They landed here, their journey but begun,
to seek false oracles from falser gods,
their lofty citadels a smoking waste
of broken visions. Out upon the sea
they set their course, and lifted up their eyes
to destinies far greater than their dreams.

What solace is this now, to us, who strive
with all the wisdom of our varied past,
so richly, yet so unavailingly
engraved within our minds. Perhaps we see
in their predestined heights, our lonely hope,
in their release our great, undreamt-of end.

AT SUMMER'S END

Now in the sweet September chill
I watch the yellowing leaf spin down
and am remembering suddenly
a summer evening warm and still:

the mellow air was pink and clear,
with pink phlox sentinel in the dusk
and in the far blue-arching sky
one sharp star standing white and near.

And now the phlox is cut away
and where the lilacs hummed with bees
the leaves hang empty, dreaming of
that drugged and scented latter day.

But ah, my heart is not afraid
and sees no threat in this decline
from sun-warmed flowers to splitting pod,
knowing it will not be betrayed.

Time is no enemy to fear.
Love knows time's secret and is glad,
and stands with wide arms, welcoming
all seasons in each friendly year.

AUTOBIOGRAPHY

This stream is subject to no stress of tide;
floods come to drag the bank and pull the willows,
and summer withers all the countryside
sometimes with drought, when these bright stones
    are dust,
this water, pure as love new and untried,
sinks to a dying rivulet of pain.

But here there is no tide, there is no ebb,
no rising, from the impressionable moon;
the brook is clear and shallow as delight
or shrinks, or is inadequate for storm;
here is no proud, awakened surge of earth,
no stir of stars, but brief perfection's dearth.

GROWTH

At what instant does the summer change?
What subtle chemistry of air
and sunlight on the clean and windsmooth sand?
    The small birds at the water's edge –
        yesterday they were not there.

So suddenly the magic door is shut,
the trio suddenly is done,
the clasped hands inexplicably apart;
    however dear, however bright,
        the road we traveled on is gone.

101

ADMONITIONS

I

Why hold your heart in quiet? Is there not
more than we comprehend within a night
clear and trembling cold, diminished moon
and thin stars high and sweet? Look out beyond,
there where the bare trees stand against the sky
and the weak bat cheeps and flutters, safe from light.
Look out beyond, and let your heart go free.
This beauty now is real, not sent to trap
and trick you into loving something, gone
before its breath has whispered on your face.
Till time immortal, nights like these shall come
to link you with the years, and sweep along
the beating rhythm of the race's song.

II

To know the moment is to know an age.
A moment to the heart of hills is nought;
an age a moment. So much less are we
than those dark mountains where the deer climb swift,
and pause to watch the valley smoke rise up

out of men's sweat into an open sky.
To know the moment is to feel an age
pulsing under the hand, yet you would pass
the long way through the woods and take the road,
leaving the sun-laced forest floor unseen,
the fairy song of thrush and ovenbird
save for attentive, brush-tailed squirrels, unheard.

102

(FOR DAVID)

Prune when winter is in the bough.
When spring holds sway
then you will say,
I cannot cut it now,
not when the blossoms' sweet
bewitching breath
speaks of the fruit to come,
and not of death.

All future autumns hang
within the seed,
and fruit less fair
will cluster there
if you deny the need
for cutting off, in winter's
numbing cold,
the limbs that will destroy you
when you're old.

ONLY A LITTLE LONGER

If we could hold the moment, hold the light
only a little longer, keep our hands
white in the sun without the shadows moving
over them slowly and the warmth destroyed;
if we could keep the woodthrush in the hollow
longer and never wake to know the hush,
the emptiness of dawn without his song,
we might have wisdom then, we might have wisdom.
But the leaves have flickered down, open to all
the secret places where the brown wings flew
within the hollow. If we yet could hold
only a little longer, light on our hands —

THE INLAND GULLS

Over this field the white gulls
float and veer,
        circle,
                drift down,
swoop off in great musical curves,
wheel back again and come in with spread wings
to settle on the brown waves of earth
where the farmer passes by.
Plow and harrow,
seed and harvest:
for them all, the gulls come in from the sea,
beating inland with morning wings,
outward again as dusk folds down
in dusk-winged flocks
to settle somewhere over the sands.

For how long has it been so,
gulls crying over the inland furrow,
gulls in the wake of the plow
as it breasts the earth's tide?

Does the man at the plow look up
and see and remember,
linked by a frail wing to all his lost brothers
who walked in these fields
before him?

There are things to be remembered
when the heart is old,
and many words are waiting
before the tale is told;
for many hawks are plunging
upon the summer air,
and still the mice are creeping,
and still the world is fair.

A necessary evil
is portioned to the heart;
we might as well acknowledge
the devil from the start
and know the hasty blossom
as swiftly will decay,
while other flowers are waiting
to grace a forward day.

It is foolish to have wisdom
and folly to be blind;
to see and take and question
must nourish any mind;
reserve a quiet judgment
until the heart is old,
when fewer words are needed
before the tale is told.

Here, on this surge of hill, I find myself
not as I am or will be or once was,
not as the measure of days defines my soul;
beyond all that a being of breath and bone,
partaker of wind and sun and air and earth,
I stand on the surge of hill and know myself.
Below, the stars sink landward, and above
I breathe with their slow glimmer; fields are gone,
the woods are fallen into the speechless dark;
no claim, no voice, no motion, no demand.

It is alone we end then and alone
we go, creatures of solitary light;
the finger of truth is laid upon my heart:
See and be wise and unafraid, a part
of stars and earth-wind and the deepening night.

PLAGUE

Now standing by the castle shaw at dusk
with golden shadows lying on the fields
and green autumnal peace across the land
who can relive the terror of those days?
The lanes deserted and the kine unfed,
the harvest waiting – never to be reaped;
the children crying for the unbaked bread
and no hands left to lay away the dead.

One man remained to rule this lonely fief.
Scarcely one life span saw this castle's use;
then it was left to weather and the owls,
the stones lugged off, the great beams pried away,
wood pigeons roosting on the rotting walls,

and now we stand beside the crumbling moat
to stare and wonder.

After a visit to Glottenham Castle, East Sussex, where the
Black Death (1300–1350) took every inhabitant but one.

THE TEACHER

What has an old heart to give to the young?
What have old eyes that have looked on the world
to share with the new eyes that see the new day?
The times I have looked on are flowing away.

All the works written and read are as naught;
all of the theorems and problems and sums
are thin as their paper and empty as air;
and all has been sullied that should have been fair.

Double-compounded the sins of the past;
we serve with our tongues what we scorn
    with our lives;
fear trammels our hearts; the earth under our feet
is dark with the sorrow no wisdom can meet.

The span of our years is as quick as the sun
that rises and sets, and our page is as brief
as it takes in the telling, and what have I seen
but the folly of all that our striving has been?

An old man, an old heart, and weary I go —
yet filled with a joy that no sorrow can quench,
for under it all runs a hope like a spring,
a harmony vaster than man can yet sing,

and I praise that beneath all the pain there is love
that gathers us into a harvest to come
more wide than the world or the sky or the sea,
a harvest of souls in the world to be.

HEARTH

From the air they filmed the shadow on the downs
near the dew pond on the leeward side,
out of the sea wind. "Worth looking at," they said
and made an X mark on their map. So now they stood
getting their bearings, setting up their gear,
waiting for the Head to have his say to where
to lay their grid, and how to start their dig.

"We need to find the hearth," at length he said,
"if what we saw we can confirm today
with our first trials. See where the barrows lie?
And see the shadows on the film, just west, below
and by this little coombe. Sometimes the sheep
they sheltered there. Let's see what we can find.
And if we find the hearth, we've found the heart of it."

They worked in weather and in centuries.
The gulls came crying over in the seaborne wind
and jackdaws stalked about to study them.
They laid back turf down to the chalk and flint,
numbered and put aside the tools, the bones:

an antler pick, an awl, crude shards of bowls, a quern,
and to one side a dog's skull – shepherd's dog? –
a mulling stone that fitted in the palm.

And then they found a circle deep in ash
set round with sea-scoured boulders from the beach
below. They stood and gazed. The years washed
    over them:
a night sky brilliant with unhindered stars,
the flicker and warmth and fellowship of fire,
and the tribe gathered round the heart of life.

A fighter jet roared in from off the sea,
curved round and vanished south – and broke the spell.
The Head looked up and sighed. "We've found their
hearth at least. My question is: Have we not lost
    our own?"

POMPEII

The columns crumble in the sunwhite streets,
dust lingers yet on everything, the same
which flooded down the writhing mountainside
into the doorways, fell from the smoking sky,
bubbled and crept across the burnished floors.
They are the same, the same, the sandaled feet,
the bodies quick with grace, dark eyes, and slim,
fine hands that cut the figures on the wall;
somewhere they are the same. Could this have gone
under the seething horror in one night?
It is a broken city now, for us
to poke around and dig the stewpots out.
"A woman prayed here when the rain-fire came.
It caught her as she knelt." "There is a loaf
some housewife had to leave while still uncut."
The stove remains, the broken fountainhead,
the mirrors and the shining jeweled rings.
Where are the warriors and the tyrant kings?
Banished, banished.

We who have come to walk the lonely streets,
to pause in the sunlight where the columns stood
cool and serene within the shadowed court,
we have returned. We have seen this before
and known it when the walls were more than dust,
the fountains springing and the bread loaves fresh.
Why else should we be called by silent stones,
the merchants and the lovers of the light,
the poets and the singers in the night,
vanished, vanished?

ABIDING

Black rooks on silver-frosted field
and white gulls flying over —
why does it catch my heart and pull
old memories out from cover?

Old weathered sheep, as twilight gathers,
drifting toward the gate,
knowing that there, as sun dips low,
their shepherd is wont to wait.

And bells across the evening meadows:
"Listen!" We stop to hear
men make the intricate design
of sound from long-past year.

The hush and draw of measured wave
on shingle and on shore —
where are the folk who ran their keels
over the beach before?

What flocks poured down this hollow lane,
with shepherd following after,
between deep-rooted ash and thorn
into a greener pasture?

Things that abide are those that God
and man have loved together:
the sheep, the keels, the bells, the bird,
the shepherd – are forever.

VI

Self-knowledge

STRUGGLE

The heart's winter,
    the soul's drought,
the mind's ice
    hardening out,
the deep clutch
    of circumstance,
the numbed spirit
    in a trance —

Oh break! oh break,
fire in the East,
that we may rise,
that we may wake!

113

(TO R . A . C .)

All day, though this is April,
the wild clouds scattered snow,
to singe with frost the flowers
that tried to thrive and grow.

All day, though this is April,
I felt the chilling air
strike at the untimely blossom
and shatter what was fair.

Now that the dark is creeping
across the thwarted earth,
I trust the uncertain morrow
to bring me back my mirth.

THE IDEALIST

Until the last brave echo seeks these hills,
I will defend the fastnesses of men
and stand before the gateway of the heart
to perish ere the vanquisher creeps in;

therefore, O Evil, count me enemy
and look for no withdrawal, no retreat;
if you would do me battle, there will be
no end but one the morning that we meet.

Within this valley I have watched the years
scatter abundant seasons as they go;
I and my comrades moved across these fields,
leaving the wheat behind us, row on row.

We loved too well to yield without a cry;
bitter or sweet, there was a glory here;
the marsh was green and rippling in the sun,
and with the whistling fall was bleak and sere.

Still it was lovely, lush with rain or old,
alike earth fed us, summertime or cold;
we looked into each other's eyes and knew
we touched the source; the spring was clear and true

and stars and rain and all the dusky wind
and music when the single day drew in
and parchment thin by firelight, and a voice,
and roads that waited our deliberate choice.

O Evil, come and take me if you can;
I guard the gateway, knowing no retreat
unto my utmost breath, and there will be
no end but one the morning that we meet.

Tell me it is enough to be as I am now,
    and young,
and filled with the dark necessity of you,
and with delight at the thin crying of a gull
    against sunlight and bright water.

Tell me it is enough,
that more is not required of me,
that I need not stain my hands with the
    world's blood
or choose which side to hate,
or give up this drift of my heart, this joy,
this insupportable joy at the gull's white cry
and your hand lifted to me.

Tell me I must not deny my life,
    for the world,
for the world's hate and the world's anger.

THE LESSON

How failure does persuade
the tough and stubborn soul
to yield the prideful role
that it has blindly played!

Oh bright humility —
Oh blessed sweet despair
that racks us till we dare
to bend the stiffened knee!

(T O R . A . C .)

Being wrong is being young; the day
that I am right I'll know that I am old.

The night the sea fails to distract my mind;
the hour I am not set adrift by sound
of music; and the moment I am caught
no longer in a web, remembering you,
then I will know that I am old at last.

Being young is being wrong; they say
wisdom is kept exclusively for age.
Yes – but I'll keep my bodkin by my side.
They'll say, so wise was she that – lo – she died.

It is not here that we may find atonement –
not here that the body may seek its hollow in the sand –
not here that the heart may settle itself for contemplation:
therefore arise again and be gone.

The night is brief and the harsh daylight sudden;
not long can the hills shadow us and hold peace –
for down the valley the light comes hunting us:
therefore arise again and be gone.

Break not the compelling motion with rebellion –
the swifter the heart goes onward without wrath
the sooner will the purpose come and the destiny:
therefore arise again with joy and be gone;
therefore be gone into the great vista, fearless.

PEOPLE OF FRANCE (1944)

The light that we have long awaited
they tell us is not far; the bitter dark
still to be bitter, while yet unabated,
holds a new promise as the ships embark.

Could we believe it, what unnamed rejoicing
would break like shepherd's flutes from every hill,
and from each cave would shout the children, voicing
farewell to the fear that waits upon them still.

Man was not made to know such happy morrows;
words such as those you speak we have forgot;
man was created to be spent with sorrows,
hunger and fireless hearth his ultimate lot.

We wait the light half-eager and half-dreading,
fearful of what the sun at last will show;
the men who bound us and the men who free us,
which face belongs to which we may not know.

TO ONE WHO BLAMES HITLER

We – all of us – bear our guilt;
like rainfall – we are together – and the flood
comes from our separate strength.

Therefore this hate is not on him,
not wholly born of his peculiar gall
which wries the world with pain.

I have seen your eyes flash with hate;
my friend, the serpent lurks within you, too.
Your venom coils and waits.

THE SHEPHERD

Well I know now the feel of dirt under the nails,
I know now the rhythm of furrowed ground under foot,
I have learned the sounds to listen for in the dusk,
the dawning and the noon.

I have held cornfields in the palm of my hand,
I have let the swaying wheat and rye run through my fingers,
I have learned when to be glad for sunlight and for sudden
thaw and for rain.

I know now what weariness is when the mind stops
and night is a dark blanket of peace and forgetting
and the morning breaks to the same ritual and the same
demands and the silence.

Oh faultless dark and final night of peace,
why is there fear possessing all my bones,
warm in my blood and quivering in my eyes?
Must all the heart's assurance sometime cease,
or is it not the certain past atones
the future's doubt? No, see, the old faith dies
and flickers out like stars before the rain,
and all the years of certainty are worn
ghosts of an early and forgotten morn,
powerless to stir the wind of dawn again.

MEDITATION

This day – sea, sunlight, laughter by my side,
gull beating on the air, gull folding wings
to plummet to the water and to rise
with a slim silver prize –

this day – alive with love and yet alive
in the same air, with hate, with fear, with tears,
and I untouched, ungiven, with no choice
but to withhold my voice.

Trammeled we are, who would deny all force,
sheltered, who would withstand all buffeting,
granted, as listeners to our deepest pleas,
the mute and patient trees.

Where is the test, the proof, of our intent!
I, in the peace of seawind with the cry
of a far suntouched gull, caught in this day,
see no immediate way.

Only a life that's hammered to the end
by one sure purpose shall at length suffice
to show the Lord the strength of my desire
to guard His eternal fire.

The great storm breaks in from the sea,
and in the end there is peace and white sunlight
and the gathering in of autumn
and rain on the earth again after the dry haze of summer
and the heart is brisk and the eyes clear
and the voice sings in the ringing air.

But it is not so with the storm you would make,
for it will leave dust in the mouth and the heart
choked with the dust of hate, and the eyes blurred;
the voice will be thick and the air shattered
and there will be no harvest but dry stalks
and the rotted grain.

THE OPTIMISTIC BORE

She is caught in a perpetual June,
the chronic vapidness of blissful weather,
and sees significance ad nauseam
in the least fleeting wing and blowing blossom,
and scatters sunshine everywhere she goes
until one thirsts most avidly for rain
and feels the blacker as she brighter grows
and hopes she will not pass one's way again.

LAMENT FROM PURGATORY

*"There is never time to say our last word – the last word
of our love, or our desire, faith, remorse, submission, revolt."*
        Joseph Conrad

The day I let the door slam to
and angry, filled the blameless street
with my disease; the day I drew
an evil line of ridicule
around that innocent awkward soul
and cut him off from fellowship
and trapped him in a scapegoat's role,
and never wiped my circle out.

The day that, melted down with love
I tried to speak, but found no word
elegant nor rich to prove
the stature of my skill, so kept
silence until it was too late.

The day I rose with righteous wrath
that simmered down to useless hate

before it could be turned to power,
transform to glory some cursed hour.

The day my faith rose up in me
and burst the bonds of mind and heart
and almost, almost set me free –
but time's incessant clamoring
stayed me from the last severing
with fear, and faith sank back again
the last word still unsaid, unsaid.

Oh blessed Lord, I meant to bring
the healing final word to these
lost treasures of thy life, to sing
as if I were thy instrument,
with thy breath pushing clear and sweet
through me into the world! Too late –

and now amid the still white stars
I cling and watch the earth spin by,
weeping to see men squandering
the golden instant, as did I.

REPENTANCE

If I could feel
that in the healing of my imperfections
thou wouldst be glorified,
if I could know
that in my weakness being by thee transformed
the world would praise thee more,
I would be not less guilty or resigned
but more zealous,
     stung
out of self-pity into pitiless action,
and praising thee for my sins
that wait thy cleansing.

Therefore descend, O fire of faith!
burn over the scrubby waste of my flat soul
that spring may bloom unhampered.

RESPONSE TO CRITICISM

Do it the way you will – I only know
that it was right for me to do it so.
Take any two right hands and clench them tight,
they will not grasp a rod with equal might –
nor will they be alike when in repose.
Two bushes never bear the selfsame rose.

So leave me scope for some experiment
in finding out just what the good Lord meant
when He created in my patient mother
this untried soul that's me and is no other.

LORD, SHOW ME THYSELF

How unsuspecting do we wait
a visitation of thy power
and heedless wander in a maze
nor reckon up the coming hour.

And when thy finger points at us
we glance behind, confused with doubt
that we are now become the one
thy tutelage has singled out.

This is the moment to deny,
to hide our faces from thy sight,
or else to stand and open wide
the doors of being to thy light.

SELF-REPROACH

My house being now at rest, the dark rooms silent,
do I have time at last to turn to thee?
Or with the closing down of all distraction
am I less driven or a whit more free?

The clear reproof in all my contemplation,
the hasty prayer (no time to bend the knee)
reveals thy face is hidden by my vigor
to crowd the landscape so I cannot see.

So thus and thus I make myself the blinder,
accumulate the duties of the days,
and fill with human kind the mystic chasm
I might have filled with thee in other ways.

And in the dark house even I have gendered
too much of this world's stir to let thee rest,
too busy at the elbows of thy creatures
to wait on thee, most high and holy guest.

THE PIT

Upward to sunlight
what tangle now still holds
the struggling feet?

Up to the clear air
the circle of heaven free,
what fear of falling
makes the threat real
so that we clutch and cannot climb?

O sweet and pure light
smelling of meadow
tangy with new-felled wood,
full of melody!

And underneath the dark, the past,
the unredeemed,
still fettering.

THE CHAIN

Too late we break the siege
of the close-bastioned heart
and find the city starved,
dry to the bone, and dark.

Too late we cut the chain,
who cannot find the key;
the captive soul has died,
the captive flame is quenched.

The devil does not thrust
against the armored gate,
nor counsels us to yield —
he counsels us to wait.

Dear Lord, forgive me
for the peddler's pack of petty sins
I carry on my back —
flimsy, tawdry trinkets
no one wants —
of no use,
neither for thy glory
nor to men.

If I could sing
like the sparrow,
or praise thee with bright wings
like the sun-seeking butterfly —
or open like a flower
in thy appointed time!

But I lug with me through the dust
this burden of self,
and spill at thy feet
small-hearted gaudiness —
not even one good, sound loaf,
however small,
to nourish another's heart.

GUILT

For all man's Palomars,
for all the far-flung gold-consuming dreams
of stepping on the stars,
of pressing out to new eternities;

for all our turning inward to the small
infinitely precious secrets in the blood,
devising ways to alter destinies –
we have forgot the Flood.

We still pluck the Apple,
    we still hide
when God walks in the Garden.

We still turn aside,
while the Child has died.

THE EMPTY HOUSE

No one comes to supper anymore,
there is no music and there is no bread,
the candle flame is out,
the hearth fire dead —
the cricket chirrs unheard.

There is no music and there is no bread,
the sparrows squabble on the broken sill.
No one returns at dusk, no voices call.
The air is dead, the rooms are cold and still,
no word is said.

(TO R . A . C .)

The seed of sorrow hides within this flower.
We who have nourished it must take the blame;
we who have turned its earth and given it name
must watch the steady passing of its hour.

But see the yew tree in the winter's cold;
remember now the spruce, the ivy's dark
approach across the snow, the cedar's stark
strong spring of green against a world gone old.

THE PATTERNED HEART

The patterned heart is stubborn to reform;
the soul desires forever its first food
and lives but briefly on a different fare;
the eye accustomed to the edge of earth
battles with hills that shut the edge from view;
the ear that listened first to silences
struggles with sound as a bird within the net.

We are not sand to shift beneath the wind,
showing new contours after every storm;
more than the blast of hate must turn my love,
more than the noise of logic change my faith;
my food was peace, my vision space, my sound
the sound of silence, and by these alone
will I be moved to come into my own.

ZACCHAEUS

Zacchaeus in a sycamore
looked upon God, who summoned him;
small man, he had to climb to see,
to forfeit human dignity.

The choice to climb is up or down,
to stretch or stoop, and either way
the self must yield and melt away
if the Lord's face we would see:
Zacchaeus found his tree.

Now breaks the ice upon the silvered branch,
the brief assault of sun sufficient grace
to crack the cold enchantment and redeem
the straining weighted form. It takes not much

of concentrated radiance to dispel
the sheaths that hold us rigid; one brief glance
of brilliant love will give sufficient heat
to start in frozen heart a tentative beat.

VII

Faith

A HILLTOP FIELD

*"Faith is the energy the Master gives you which enables you
to take hold of His promises and to participate in His life."*
        Phillipe Vernier

Faith has no abode, no tree-hid haven,
no rock-encircled harbor where the tide
will never swirl nor threaten; nor has faith
the quiet breast of broad sweet-flowing river.

Faith has a hilltop field alive and growing,
faith has its nets staked out in open sea,
faith is a rocky river, swift and harnessed
to fill the valley with its energy.

I wait no destiny, I am convinced;
I stir no hands, I light no eyes from mine,
nor will my music ever shake the stars,
my words turn years to leaves before the wind.

I am the listener always, and no more;
I take my light from others, and my hands
move at another's bidding, and my voice
echoes the words I can not claim my own.

Oh, but I share the consciousness of breath;
I have my purpose – I fulfill my days.
Somewhere within me is the invulnerable flame
which hissed and flared the day man first took fire
and stirred and woke, and knew his first desire.

142

HARVEST

I shall believe in sorrow when it comes
like the first down-wandering of snow,
laying its drift of shadow on my heart,
hugging against the hedges of my soul,
gathering on the lintel of my door.

Its wide and still possession of the air
I shall acknowledge as necessity
and pray and pray, not for an early spring
but for the harvest that the year must bring.

Bird on the bare branch,
flinging your frail song
on the bleak air,
tenuous and brave —
like love in a bleak world,
and like love,
pierced
with everlastingness!

O praise
that we too
may be struck through with light,
may shatter the barren cold
with pure melody
and sing
for thy sake
till the hills are lit with love
and the deserts come
to bloom.

QUERY

How is the harvest of the heart today,
when all the hills are flaming with the fall
and the wind fills with scarlet spinning down?

What is love's harvest as the frost sets in?
Is hearth wood gathered, pine cones in the bin
to flame with blue and gold in winter's cold?

And has the wheat been milled, so that the flour
is ready for the leaven and the loaf?
Is the heart quick, to answer to the hour?

Mother of sorrows, look upon me now.
There is a heart within my heart, and eyes
within my eyes; oh, say upon my brow
some measure of your certain blessing lies.
Soon enough this pulse will beat alone,
new and unsure within a stranger land,
sharing the exile of our flesh and bone,
watching for sign of some uplifted Hand.
Grant me your grace now to be unafraid,
instill within me music and some peace
so that upon the child there will be laid
already joy before it seeks release,
so that its share of breath is full of light
and will be rich and strong before the night.

There is not the rush of wind in this love
nor is there the wild pound and surge of sea
    on shore;
but I stand fearless with it
    and certain,
my hand on the source of all things:
tremor of furled leaf out of the earth,
sough and fall of wheat under the stroke
    in the heavy field.

I am fulfilled, am taken into the earth's heart
    by this love;
I have my meaning complete;
there is no more question.

THE SPIDER

I watch the spider fling
its most improbable thread –
frail filament
yet steel strong –
from aspen limb to birch
and back again.

So do we fling our faith
from star to star
and under God's eternal, watching care
the perfect orb
will come.

Out of a difficult and troubled season
the timely harvest thrusts amid the stones;
the dry mind that would claim a thousand reasons
melts beneath the Lord's appointed rain.

The furred magnolia buds we bring to warmth
here in the heated room soon bloom and sicken;
the tree without keeps its own secret time.

Powerless are we to move God with our clamor,
to seize the least fringe of His mystery;
but we must wait until the gift is given
and poor, walk faithfully the lanes of heaven.

RESOLVE

I'll wash my hands of innocence
and cast the snowy robe aside
and shun the face of purity
to walk where sinners now abide.

The bare and brutal face of hate
I must go forth to look upon
and clasp the hand of treachery
with love as if it were my own.

My sins are inward and refined,
my friends the gentle friends of God;
I must go seek the publicans,
the wild companions of my Lord.

THE MASTER

He who has come to men
dwells where we cannot tell
    nor sight reveal him,
until the hour has struck
when the small heart does break
    with hunger for him;

those who do merit least,
those whom no tongue does praise
    the first to know him,
and on the face of earth
the poorest village street
    blossoming for him.

WOODCREST

Who walks beside the hemlocks on this lane,
whose shoulders brush the sumac on the slope
climbing to see the valley flowing out
and the dark folds beyond it, hill on hill?

Upon whose ears does all our music fall?
Whose hand is laid upon our children's heads?
And as the saw bites through the measured wood,
for whose sake do we stand here laboring?

And in the cold with all the world in need,
for whose sake do we open wide the door?
Who lights the fire that gives us energy
and makes of our poor strength His lasting home?

♦ FAITH

THE GATE

No one compels you, traveler;
this road or that road, make your choice!
Dust or mud, heat or cold,
fellowship or solitude,
foul weather or a fairer sky,
the choice is yours as you go by.

But here if you would take this path
there is a gate whose latch is love,
whose key is single and which swings
upon the hinge of faithfulness,

and none can mock, who seeks this way
the king we worship shamelessly.
If you would enter, traveler,
into this city fair and wide,
it is forever and you leave
all trappings of the self outside.

CONVERSION

Defenseless, Lord, by thee I am defended;
blind, by thy borrowed senses do I see;
trapped by offenses that are never ended,
by thy sweet discipline am I set free.

Stung to contrition, I have been forgiven;
sick, by thy wholeness now have I been healed.
Though by my sin thy blameless heart was riven,
still by thy love is my salvation sealed.

So may I be possessed and claimed and altered,
no part of life denied but all transferred
into thy kingdom where no man has faltered
but to be raised again by thy sure word.

So may I live, that men may know the witness
and see the light reflected from thy face;
may I not question my own strength or fitness
but trust the eternal promise of thy grace.

BAPTISM

Plowman, down the narrow field
that reaches out beyond the sun,
through me let your furrow run.

Sower, striding on the earth
along the furrows newly made,
within me let the seed be laid.

Harvester of all that's fair,
let me full and purely grow
that you may cut and lay me low.

THE NEW DISCIPLE

The Beginning
Pure as a child the day is newly born;
fresh from thy love the hours of light are given.
So let me rise and turn my face to thee,
newly created as the unblemished morn.

The Middle
Under the press of noon still may I go,
my hand in thine wherever I may wander,
all noise and tumult, labor and distress
powerless to draw me from the path I know.

The End
And when thy day is growing dim and old,
weary but steadfast may I homeward turning,
find thy fire glowing, know myself to be
thy true lamb gathered safely in thy fold.

THE BLESSED MEEK

I

Who scorns the lifted hand of God,
who woos revenge and curses fate,
he rides the stallion of hate.

Who spits upon the fertile sod
and casts faith's tiny seedlings out,
he rides the stallion of doubt.
Who beats himself with pity's rod
and blames his life on circumstance,
he rides the stallion of chance.

The crooked road and treacherous way,
the marshmud sucking at the hoof,
the thickly tangled, thieving wood,
the burst into the blinding day –
the Devil tramples at our side
who join that dusty, furious ride.

II

Deliver me, deliver me,
O Lord, who rode a lowly beast!
　　May I ride meekly to thy feast,
　　and gently jog through sun and shade
　　and see the pattern of each field
　　counting the blessing of its yield
　　and love each leaf that thou hast made,
and wait with peace the dazzling light,
the final, swift, eternal flight,
the sweet dark channels of the night.

THE MIRACLE

"And to be true, and to speak my soul, when I survey the
occurrences of my life and call into account the Finger of
God, I can perceive nothing but an abyss and mass of mer-
cies. Those which others term crosses, afflictions, judgments,
misfortunes — to me they both appear and in event have
ever proved the dissembled favors of His affections."
                    Sir Thomas Browne

Pity me not. You do not know
the hidden emblem that I bear,
nor the bright crown of circumstance
that all invisible I wear.

I cannot now communicate
the lesson that my soul absorbs,
nor, taught so tenderly of God,
can I yet translate into words

why what is bondage to the world
becomes a labor freely done,
that what I would have called a grief
is grief and rapture bound in one.

In sorrow's season the heart finds
the Lord does but reveal His face,
and what held terror to the soul
becomes a miracle of Grace.

VANITAS VANITATUM

The pale heart waits the flow of outward strength;
always our faces in the ambient night
seek the clear flood of a redeeming light,
and the dark surface breaks with sun at length.

Nothing we do, we do ourselves alone;
the peace of love is learned, the use of pain;
beauty falls on us like the lash of rain;
wisdom will touch us and become our own.

Now a wild earth groans with great disease,
the wide thunder breaks and wind breeds wind;
we cry out on others who have sinned
and clutch their guilt to us in faulty ease.

Dear Lord, have mercy on us in this hour.
Teach us that never will the soul be free
till it has known itself athirst for thee,
voiceless and dim, but for thy ultimate power.

PRAYER

Oh, break the chrysalis of doubt,
plow up the clods of thick despair,
and split the buds of ignorance,
and cleanse the winter-heavy air!

Create a tumult in our hearts,
drive us to seek what we have lost,
until the flame of faith again
has seared us with thy Pentecost!

THE PROMISE

I who have sinned against God
stand cold and empty-handed,
desert under my feet
with no hope of flowering,
athirst where there is no spring,
in a land where no manna falls
and no voice speaks –

Ah, but somewhere
my brother loves me,
from far, from unknown places
my brother speaks for me,
my brother calls me,
my brother longs with a pure love
to break the spell of the barren land,
to rend the dry earth that binds me –

Then from the vast, brassy, barren sky
comes the small cloud,
the gathering sweet rain.

Then comes the warm wind
and the sound of bells,
the sound of running feet
and glad voices calling;
the flowers spring up and the birds
beat with glad wings about my shoulders.

And a child takes my hand, crying,
Come – the Kingdom awaits!

SUBMISSION
(FOR MONA)

Let my heart lie fallow in the sun,
let the grasses bloom, the small birds come,
the field mouse raise her brood, the cricket sing,
the joyful lark rise upward in the spring.

Let my heart lie fallow in thy name,
who bore our sin and carried all our shame.
Then will the Plowman cleave a richer sod;
then will the grain be harvested for God.

MAGNIFICAT

I thank thee, Lord, that if I die in this,
it will be too much, not too little living,
that I have sunk beneath too heavy fruit,
not withered in a desert far from thee.
Glory to thee, Lord, that thou dost give
harvest so lavish our arms cannot hold
nor heart contain the treasure of thy power.

And in the end forgive if I am proud
to go down blest by more than I can bear,
inadequate to carry out thy will,
inadequate and weak, but chosen still.

L'ENVOI

For Christ's sake now it should be joy to part,
and the long flight that bears thee far away
and my deep-grounded vigil day by day
should knit and heal and blend, not cleave our heart.

What matter if we see the mornings break
and watch the long nights flickering by alone?
Time's weariness, soul's fret can all be borne
and used with joy, if it is for Christ's sake.

Oh seek – while the hills remain.
God calls, though daylight fails,
the cruel, the pitiful, the proud,
the weak, the brave, the covetous,
the faltering, the wise, the poor,
the kings, the lepers, and the crowd.

Struck through with death, we hold the seed;
life springs, though our pale roots are dry;
though heaven never seemed so high,
God stoops, to touch our need.

And all the ages fall away;
eyes meet, and shoulders touch at last;
Christ waits, and gathers in His day
the present, future, and the past.

HOPE

Heaven is above me
no matter where I be:
in the depths of sorrow,
in the depths of sea.

In the mines of evil,
in the pits of sin,
Heaven is above me
and the Light creeps in.

Heaven is never sleeping
though my heart is dead,
though my soul is rotten
and all love has fled.

I cannot hide from Heaven,
I cannot hide from Light,
for lo, the Light will seek me
down the streets of Night.

There is no fleeing from it
no matter where I be;
above is always Heaven
and Heaven is finding me.

FOR THOSE
WHO FOLLOW THE ROAD

Out of the darkened earth the seed still springs;
the root of love is strong all bonds to burst.
The hour will come; the new time will break forth,
yes, even now the joyful news still rings.

We link our hands across the vanished past;
the road is long but thronged with travelers.
Each victory shines clear, however small;
all victories will blaze as one at last

into the great and all-consuming light,
burning away the sin of every heart.
The sorrow of the ages is redeemed.
The Lord will come in majesty and might!

FAITH

You who have watched the wings of darkness lifting
and heard the misted whisper of the sea,
shelter your heart with patience now, with patience,
and keep it free.

Let not the voiced destruction and the tumult
urge to a lesser prize your turning mind;
keep faith with beauty now, and in the ending
stars you may find.

We shall be circled over at length
  by a remoter sky,
and flung into a starrier space
  more deep, more high.

Some day the little mind of man
  will crack and spin
to let the chattering years fly out,
  forever in.

The sea will be more brief to us
  than jewel of rain;
and what now stuns us with its might,
  beauty or pain,

will be as faint as cheep of mouse
  or swing of flower
under the gusty wing of heaven;
  and what seems power

will drop away and pale to dust
    held in the palm;
and what seems passion now will sink
    to leveled calm.

Therefore be quiet with your breath,
    all little men,
and hold some wonder, in the Now
    for the great Then.

When this whole wide valley fails,
when man's fragile peace is gone
and earth's fickle day is done,
His great heart is burning on.

While our sun is flaming out
and all its worlds are pulled along
to crumble in eternal dawn,
we travel homeward to His heart.

When the abyss of time is spanned,
the circling aeons melt away
into a nameless, unknown day,
He holds us still within His hand.

CHRIST THE SHEPHERD

O Shepherd, on the hills of light,
in the far pastures where we stray,
may thy voice lead the flock aright
through perilous and stony way.

May all the lone and scattered sheep
who wander far and heedless roam
through valley dark and hillside steep
hear thy voice calling, and come home.

And may we to one fold be turned,
all at thy bidding gathered in,
and where of old thy watchfires burned
may new fires leap and flare again.

O Shepherd, on the hills of light,
may we acknowledge thee alone
who holds us through the bitterest night
and always, always calls us home.